COLLIER COUNTY LEGAL

"FIGHTING BACK!"

TO WHOM THIS MAY CONCERN – ANY AND ALL DETAILS CONTAINED IN THIS CHRONICLE WERE RESEARCHED FROM PUBLICLY AVAILABLE SOURCES IN THE YEARS OF 2016 THROUGH APRIL 2020. THE CONTENT OF THIS BOOK HAS BEEN WRITTEN AS NARATIVE NON-FICTION OBSERVATION OF THE EXECUTION OF FLORIDA STATE LAWS AND STATUTES WITHIN COLLIER COUNTY'S MISDEMEANOR LEGAL SYSTEM.

CHARACTERS NAMES HAVE BEEN CHANGED.

Additionally, thank you for all the Vanderbilt Beach and Naples Park Citizens who contributed to this book. With your stories, none of what has been written would have come to light to be shared.

<u>CONTENTS</u>

COLLIER COUNTY LEGAL

"FIGHTING BACK"!

COLLIER COUNTY LEGAL

"FIGHTING BACK"!

FORWARD

I am so tired of the flyovers by Collier County Sherriff's Office (CCSO) helicopters above my house at night. I live in the 34108 (zip code). The helicopters circle above and around Naples Park, I assume looking for someone. This type of surveillance never took place in past cities I have lived in such as Plano (Dallas), West Seattle, Nashville, Cincinnati, Columbus and Long Island, NY.

Not at Alki Beach, bordering the city of Seattle or Bozeman, Montana have this occurred.

So, why does it transpire above Naples Park and North Naples, Florida? Is it really, not safe to live here, or is there another reason?

Adding to my frustration are the, "drive-byes" by CCSO deputies in front of my house. Or seeing friends being arrested after a CCSO stop for, "Probable Cause Event", such as a license plate light not being illuminated correctly. My friends and yours, work and live here in Collier County, then why are we being punished for doing so?

The opinion of many Naples Park inhabitants of Collier County, feel the Collier County Sherriff's Office (CCSO) Deputies use a predatory approach of "Probable Cause" to arrest, penalize, and fine its hard-working tax paying Citizens.

This will be a book of discovery for some, questions for others, all based on details, data, and facts. It is up to the reader to ask themselves, is a question truly an inquiry or is it a statement?

Arrests of the Citizens of Collier County based on a law enforcement tactic called, "Probable Cause", is what **Collier County Legal – "Fighting Back"** is about and I am for one, here to tell you about it.

Those of you who think you are safe from the CCSO and it's use of, "Probable Cause Events", may be if you are a tourist, a seasonal resident or you live south of 5th Avenue in Naples. The words that will follow are from interviews with numerous citizens and they cast a dark shadow of truth for those who have yet to be arrested based on a CCSO use of

"Probable Cause". This tactic for many of Citizens of Collier County, it will be the very first time they will see the, "other side" of law enforcement. The one that does not look anything like a community parade, on Facebook, or an officer working at a school.

You might be asking yourself, what is this, "Probable Cause", this writer is referring to? It follows:

____

The 2019 Florida Statutes – Criminal Procedure and Corrections - Probable Cause

Florida Statute 901.151:

(1)   This section may be known and cited as the "Florida Stop and Frisk Law."

(2)   Whenever any law enforcement officer of this state encounters any person under circumstances which reasonably indicate that such person has committed, is committing, or is about to commit a violation of the criminal laws of this state or the criminal ordinances of any municipality or

county, the officer may temporarily detain such person for the purpose of ascertaining the identity of the person temporarily detained and the circumstances surrounding the person's presence abroad which led the officer to believe that the person had committed, was committing, or was about to commit a criminal offense.

(3) No person shall be temporarily detained under the provisions of subsection (2) longer than is reasonably necessary to affect the purposes of that subsection.

Such temporary detention shall not extend beyond the place where it was first affected or the immediate vicinity thereof.

(4)   If at any time after the onset of the temporary detention authorized by subsection (2), probable cause for arrest of person shall appear, the person shall be arrested. If, after an inquiry into the circumstances which prompted the temporary detention, no probable cause for the arrest of the person shall appear, the person shall be released.

(5)   Whenever any law enforcement officer authorized to detain temporarily any person under the provisions of subsection (2) has probable cause to believe that any person whom the officer has temporarily detained, or is about to detain temporarily, is armed with a dangerous weapon and therefore offers a threat to the safety of the officer or any other person, the officer may search such person so temporarily detained only to the extent necessary to disclose, and for the purpose of disclosing, the presence of such weapon.

If such a search discloses such a weapon or any evidence of a criminal offense it may be seized.

(6) No evidence seized by a law enforcement officer in any search under this section shall be admissible against any person in any court of this state or political subdivision thereof unless the search which disclosed its existence was authorized by and conducted in compliance with the provisions of subsections (2)-(5).

A question about the second (2) point contained in the Florida Statute 901.151, "Florida Stop and Frisk Law", is, "how does an officer know from a minor infraction that another crime may have been committed or will be committed"? Are the Deputy Sheriffs, "telepathic soothsayers"?

(2) Whenever any law enforcement officer of this state encounters any person under circumstances which reasonably indicate that such person has committed, is committing, or is about to commit a violation of the criminal laws of this state or the criminal ordinances of any municipality or county,

the officer may temporarily detain such person for the purpose of ascertaining the identity of the person temporarily detained and the circumstances surrounding the person's presence abroad which led the officer to believe that the person had committed, was committing, or was about to commit a criminal offense.

As stated, this book is written in a narrative non-fiction format. To understand its content, think about the impacts presented and what the future may bring due to this form of focused, determined persecution of the Citizens of this county.

There are eight short stories included that range from possible harassment of a U.S. Marine Veteran, "Probable Cause" stops of a bicycle rider, a blue – collar worker, a child and a hellish story of an arrest and punishment.

The point of sharing these accounts and additional subject matter is to, "shine a bright light" on the predatory approach the CCSO uses to arrest, penalize, and fine the hard-working tax paying citizens of Collier County.

From the data revealed it appears the CCSO does not seem employ the same tactics with its seventy – five thousand (75,000) seasonal inhabitants from December through April. During the same period there also is an annual influx of tourists, which can be as many as two hundred thousand (200,000) in the months of February and March.

Why are they not targeted? Is it, "Bad for Business" maybe, in a tourist driven residential community?

What qualifies me to bring these issues to the public, I have served recently as an analyst and employee for Collier County Government for six and a half years and have been on the receiving end of a, "Probable Cause" arrest.

In the past three (3) years, I have seen over thirty-eight (38) friends of mine that live in our neighborhood, Naples Park, the 34108-zip code that have been stopped by the CCSO for a, "Probable Cause" event leading to their apprehension and arrests. Teachers, construction workers, public servants, nurses, artists, entrepreneurs, business owners just to name a few, have fallen victim to this tactic used to generate arrests.

As said, **Collier County Legal "FIGHTING BACK!" (CCLFB)**, is a story that needs shared with full unadulterated disclosure to the public that loves living and visiting Collier County, though does not know how they are being influenced. **"CCLFB"**, is additionally stoked with data about racism and intolerance in Collier County.

This narrative is objective truth with facts provided to show the Collier County Sherriff's Department could possibly target and arrest county citizens based on race, class, exploiting "Probable Cause Events" to ruin lives. Furthermore, the story includes commentary associated with the legal system, trials, punishment, and for one even being a witness to *a beating of a suspect in the county jail by correction officers (Law Enforcement Officers or LEOs) prior to having his, "First Appearance" before a District Judge.*

All described above takes place in what fulltime residents, seasonal residents and tourists are led to believe are one of the best places to live, work and play in America.

For some, that statement is true, though for others, the providers of necessary services, not so much.

Naples, Florida, and Collier County has been awarded the #1 Happiest, Healthiest U.S. City by Gallup-Heathway's State of American Well-Being Community in 2017. Other awards for the wonderful pitch of land include ranked #1 Least Polluted City in U.S by Realtor.com, Conde Nast Traveler named it the 8th "Best Big City" in the U.S, was voted #9 Best Small-Town Food Scene by USA Today. Travago.com ranked it #10 the Best City for Hotels and the Recreational Fishing & Boating Foundation named Everglades National Park #1 Family Fishing Destination.

Additionally, in Forbes 2016 survey of "Best Places for Business and Careers", Collier County ranked 73rd among the nation's 200 large metropolitan areas.

I will admit that I was a fan of Naples and traveled here as a vacationer in the years of 1981, 84', 85', 86', 92', 94' , 95', 96' and relocated here as a resident in 2012.

Living and vacationing though are two radically different concepts.

Again, why **Collier County Legal "Fighting Back"**?

Just imagine how you would feel after you have been arrested based on, "Probable Cause", adjudged guilty, spending eight thousand dollars in fines and penalties.

All earnings from your employment with the Collier County Board of Commissioners.

Or, to see your own child harassed with a, "Probable Cause" stop by a Collier County Deputy Sherriff and lastly, three years after your own arrest, when your name is "Googled", your face still appears on the Internet as an, "Inmate at the Collier County Jail". The truth needs be told, and this is it.

As you read through this reveal, please keep in mind, the primary role for the contract the CCSO have with the County Citizens is to; ***Preserve and Protect the Lives, Property and Constitutional Guarantees <u>of All Persons</u>.***

You know "The Season's" over when the snowbird's autos, SUVs and exotics are being loaded to car carriers to make their way back the Midwest and Northeastern part of the US. By May, the great migration ends, and it appears that is when the Collier County Sheriff's Traffic Division begins their annual pursuit for Collier County Citizens traffic code violations. The "quest" continues through November, seven (7) months. The data to be presented is based on a four (4) year study (2016 – 2020).

The Collier County Sherriff Office (CCSO) sends its Deputy Sherriff's to prey upon their neighbors using motorcycle speed traps on US 41 from Pine Ridge Road north to Vanderbilt Road. CCSO, "unmarked" Ford, "Ghost" cars are dedicated to a Driving Under the Influence (DUI) "Task Force".

Collier County owned Ford (and Chevy) pickup trucks made out to look like personal vehicles park at Vanderbilt Beach, and the all-important Ford Escapes and Explorer SUVS that stalk looking for, "Probable Cause" events in Naples Park, Naples Manor, Golden Gate City and Parkway, Immokalee, Airport Pulling roadway and Everglades City.

The southwest coast of Florida and Collier County are chock full of Deputy Sheriffs, Judges and Lawyers here to make sure the law of the land is upheld.

Based on the arrest data, race appears to be a factor along with where a possible future inmate lives. Especially so, for those earning less than the average median income in Collier County of $68,300".

Why those demographics appear most effected, could be to stay in their own neighborhoods and to not cast a shadow on the lives to the 34102 (5th Avenue South)?

Go online yourself, to the Collier County Sheriff's Daily Arrest Reports, to observe who was arrested the previous night.

Try to find a white professional's picture/mug shot from the 34102. Not much there, huh?

The Collier County citizens besieged from a recent 30-day study over the holidays in 2019 into 2020 (DEC 20, 2019 through JAN 20, 2020) yielded the following data.

Based on five hundred and twenty-three (523) arrests.

30.4% of arrests (*) were citizens of <u>Hispanic or Latino</u> descent, though they make up **27.2% of**

the population (**)! An **11.8% out of balance**

distinction.

16.8% percent of arrests (*) were of <u>African

American</u> origin, though they make up **6.8% of the**

population (**)! A **147.1% out of balance**

distinction.

52.8% percent of arrests (*) were of

Caucasian origination, and they make up 63.6% (**)

of the population. A 16.9% reduction in arrests

versus population?

In a CCSO arrest and incarceration study conducted from February and March 2019 yielded 880 arrests (*) and they reconfirm the data from December (2019) and January (2020). The February and March 2019 numbers are detailed in the next paragraph.

27.9% (*) arrested were of Hispanic or Latino origin, 18.2% (*) were of African American descent and 52.8% (*) were Caucasians.

In the data from February and March 2019, the areas of the county appear to have more arrest activity, than others were:

East Naples (zip code-34112) with 9.8% of arrests.

South Naples (zip code-34113) with 6.4% of arrests.

Immokalee (zip code-34142) with 11.5% of arrests.

27.7% of arrests come from three (3) zip codes out of more than twenty (20) in Collier County.

Comparing to County-wide Household Income of $68,300, the average household income for the areas on the previous page were:

East Naples (34112)	$44,432	-53.7%
South Naples (34113)	$48,281	-41.4%
Immokalee (34142)	$27,760	-146.1%

(*) The arrests were provided by the daily CCSO online reporting of previous day activity that ended with incarceration. Data includes the zip codes (***) which delineate location in Collier County.

(**) The population figures are from American Fact Finder (AFF), US Census reporting from 2013 through 2017.

(****) Income data was sourced from American Community Services (ACS), US Census reporting 2019.

(*****) NAHB, News-and-Economics, Housing, Economics, Indices, Housing-Opportunity-Index

It appears from the factual data presented on the previous pages that in Collier County, those who were arrested may be because of their race or nationality, family income and or lack of it, and those that have no additional funds to defend themselves and after found guilty, leaving years of interest and payments.

Citizens who are of the wealthy "1%", or tourist or seasonal resident are not targeted, or it seems that way due to the daily arrest records.

Are the results of this type of law enforcement, including fines imposed on the disadvantaged from convictions used as a method to "keep the unfortunates" in their place"?

An unwritten policy that divides all the Citizens of Collier County and that story is the most telling of all.

Living conditions in Collier County range from migrant's farmworkers in trailers in Immokalee six (6) to seven (7) persons per housing unit.

If you earn $30,000 per year, you can work in Collier County, but when you are done each day, you go back to Lee, Charlotte, and Hendry county due to the lack of affordable housing.

The countywide new home impact fees and the way they are calculated provide inventive to developers to build housing that is $400,000 or more in value, far above what someone can afford on a thirty-thousand-dollar salary. Two income families even struggle to pay a mortgage on that amount ($2,000 a month plus taxes and insurance).

If you do not stay living out of the county there is another method to encourage you to not live in Collier County. As previously stated, that would be the Collier County Legal system and the Sheriff's use of, "Probable Cause Events", to produce arrests.

The unwritten mode of enforcement leading to segregation of those who have plenty and those who have little.

As an owner of a car dealership, when told of my own experience of earning a Collier County DUI, he said, "a DUI in Collier County is a damn tax *and* a cost of living here". So sad, though appears true.

Probable Cause

Common thread…

Actual samples of "Probable Cause" stops used by the Collier County Deputy Sherriff's in Naples Park to detain tax paying citizens –

*Walking on 101st street (at night).

*Riding a bicycle (at night).

*Riding a bicycle that does not have illuminated a front or back light.

*Driving on 8th Avenue (at night).

*Double pump on the brakes at a stop sign.

*"Rolling" through a stop sign regulated Intersection.

*One bulb not functioning on a trailer.

*Turn signals not being used.

*License plate lenses that are, "too dark".

*"Too dark" of window tint.

Do any of those "Probable Cause" events above sound, "suggestive" in nature versus "objective"?   Or something you have seen a "tourlst" or a "seasonal resident", perform?

We have provided eight acts of "Probable Cause" used by the CCSO in just one neighborhood in Collier County and there are probably more reasons to give county sheriffs the "why" to pull over you and me.

I used to love this place, until I fell victim to, "Probable Cause".

Once in a great while, a soon to be victim of "Probable Cause" will get set free, when they have been pulled over. Allowed to leave the scene of their, "stop", WHAT?

Especially so, when they have the correct job

with Collier County Government, and just happen to

be driving a county-owned vehicle.

Eight, "Probable Cause" Events

in the 34108 (Naples Park)

A walk home...

In 2017, a fellow we will call, "Shock Locks", was walking home from a restaurant located on US 41, Tamiami Trail. His journey that evening took him to 101st avenue headed west towards his house.

As he neared the intersection of 8th street north and 101st, Shock Locks noticed a CCSO Deputy Sherriff pulling up to make a stop at the same intersection.

The Deputy did not stop and made a left turn placing his standard issue white Ford sedan directly in the path Shock Locks was walking. 101st does not have sidewalks, so Shock Locks was proceeding on the left side of the road and was stunned to find he now had a fully lighted Sherriff's cruiser parked facing directly in front of him. The Deputy got out of the car and told Shock Locks to stop and stand where he was. The Deputy then approached Shock Locks and motioned him to face the front of the car with his hands on the hood.

Shock Locks complied with the Deputy, though asked why he was being stopped. The Deputy turned Shock Locks around from the hood of the Ford to face him and answered to Mr. Locks with, "where are you going? Followed by, "where have you been? "Home and dinner", Shock Locks replied.

"Well, you look like you have been drinking, have you been"? the Deputy asked. "No", Locks replied and continued with, "it's not against the law to have a drink".

The Deputy looked into Shock Locks brown

eyes, apparently searching for a reply. "It is if you

are intoxicated and stumbling home", the Deputy

continued. "I am not stumbling, have not been

drinking and am just walking home", Shock Locks

replied. The Deputy muttered something back at

Mr. Locks and motioned him to proceed with a flip

of his hand.

A bicycle ride...

In October of 2019, a fellow we will call, "Fin", decided to borrow his friend's bicycle to ride to his house, a couple of blocks away. The time was around midnight, the weather was good and the moon full providing extra light on the street.

As Fin rode the bicycle on 7th street, he came to 101st avenue when a CCSO Deputy pulled up behind him at the intersection and turned on his overhead, "flashing" lights. The Deputy motioned Fin to his vehicle as he got out of the patrol car.

After requesting Fin's name, the Deputy began his interrogation with a question.

"Mr. Fin, do you know why I stopped you", to which Fin replied, "No, I don't". The Deputy continued, stating, "I stopped you, because you do not have the red light on the back of your bike illuminated. Were you aware of this?" "No, I was not aware", Fin replied.

The Deputy observed Fin's movements and asked if he had been drinking. Fin said he had been a friend's house and had been watching a sporting match.

The Deputy went on to ask Fin if he wanted to provide a "Field Sobriety Test", that could be conducted right there, then. Fin replied, "No" to the request and the Deputy promptly arrested Fin for a, "Driving Under the Influence" or a "DUI with a Bicycle".

Fin was placed in the back of the patrol car and driven to the Collier County Jail Center on Airport Pulling Road. On the way to jail, the Deputy, stopped by Fin's friend where his trip began on 106th Avenue. The Deputy returned the bicycle there.

The question is, how did the Deputy know where Fin's friend lived, the exact address? Has that address been a target by the CCSO for observation and if so, why then?

On the trip to the jail, Fin continued attempting to have a conversation with the Deputy, but Deputy showed no interest in such. Fin was charged with Principal 316.193 (2) (A)1A DUI 1St Offense for a Bicycle.

Five months later (February 2020), Fin would accept a plea of "No Contest" to, "Disorderly Intoxication in Public Place Causing Disturbance".

Fin received no sentence other than a fine of $270 dollars.

During the five months, Fin paid a private attorney over two thousand dollars ($2,000) and endured through two arraignments in three weeks, two pre-trials, and two hearings. With Fin's plea acceptance of a lesser charge, the "Adjudication was Withheld".

Why was five (5) months of time and money wasted in pursuit of a, "Bicycle DUI" involving a County Citizen?

Was this due to action involving the State of Florida, "Stop and Frisk" Statute, Point 2, which reads, *"circumstances which reasonably indicate that such person has committed, is committing, or is about to commit a violation of the criminal laws of this state"*.

"Go back to Russia"

On a Thursday evening at 7:00pm, a friend named, "Sven" of a local business owner and entrepreneur named, "Axel", experienced a seizure and passed out. A Collier County Paramedic team were notified and appeared shortly their after at Axel's home on 106th avenue in Naples Park. Before the Paramedic's arrived, three Deputies of the CCSO also came to Axel's residence. Axel wondered why the deputies had appeared.

The Deputy Sheriff's ignored the man with the seizure lying on the carpet Axel's friend Sven and proceeded to inspect the home. No warrant for the search was presented to Axel.

Each bedroom was searched, and a small amount of marijuana was found in one of them. With Florida being a state where medical marijuana is legal, the next few aspects of the evening's CCSO behaviors are interesting at best.

As the paramedics arrived, performed services, and stabilized Sven with loading him into the ambulance.

The CCSO Deputy Sheriffs departed though not before one of the Deputy's stated to Axel, *"Go back to Russia"*. "Go back to Russia", Axel said to himself and asked, "why would I do that, I am from Sweden".

At 8:30pm, friends of Axel's, Fin and Zeph were standing outside Axel's house talking about the events they had just witnessed, when five (5) CCSO Patrol SUV's pulled up and quickly parked in front of Axel's home.

A dozen or so officers departed the vehicles each dressed what could be called "tactical or SWAT styled gear including body armor and automatic weapons". Axel commented later the next day about his experience, "what were they going to do, shoot up my house"?

In one hours, time two groups of CCSO Deputy Sherriff's responded to a, "noise complaint".

NO Search Warrants were presented.

____

A failed taillight, again with the same

Deputy that arrested Fin...

BD had been out, "boating on the Gulf" on a Sunday afternoon and when the sunset, he captained to the boat ramp at Wiggins Pass State Park. Once re-trailering his boat and leaving the park, it was less than two miles (1.7) home. One traffic light, a right turn, proceed a quarter mile to a left turn on 107th Avenue, three stop signs intersections and home. Maybe in time for a BBQ.

At 7:54pm, the same CCSO Deputy, who had stopped a friend of BD's, Fin for a taillight violation was driving northbound on Vanderbilt Drive in the 34108, when he saw BD's pick-up truck, boat and trailer coming southbound.

The ever-vigilant Deputy upon seeing a taillight light was not functioning on the trailer, made a U-turn and pursued violator BD as he made a left turn onto the street he lives on, 107th Avenue N. The Deputy followed with a left turn onto 107th Avenue and promptly stopped BD. The Deputy explained why he had stopped BD and in doing so from observation of BD's responses to his questions, began the accusatory questioning and testing leading to a DUI charge for BD.

This is where similarities between Fin (bicycle and taillight) and BD's (trailer and taillight) arrest get interesting.

Both, "Probable Cause" stops were in October 2019, conducted by the same Deputy, in the same neighborhood (Naples Park), for the same reason (taillights), and lead to the same type of arrests (DUI).

Both citations led to six (6) months to reach a final trial and for BD, he also went through multiple pre-trials (4) at considerable private attorney costs and public expenditure. It is worth noting that at this time (April 1, 2020), BD's case has not been seen for judgement.

While these men awaited trail, they both posted a bond as to not sit In the Collier County Jail.

When a "suspect" posts a, "bond" there are conditions you must agree to uphold. One of the most important, is to not get arrested again.

If arrested for an additional offense, it is not a good thing and may (for sure) impact the trial of a first offense. I do not about you, but given the CCSO's use of, "Probable Cause", the odds of another citation being received by a "suspect" in a five to six-month period appears quite likely.

Please keep in mind, I am not an attorney and any commentary I make, should not be considered as a legal opinion. Just an opinion of one.

One more failed bulb leads to another...

In 2018, MM was driving to her home on 107th just after sunset. When she made her right turn from 6th street onto 107th, she noticed a Collier County Sheriff that had been stopped at the intersection was now in her center mirror behind her.

She used her left turn signal to alert the Deputy Sherriff of her pending turn into her driveway and upon making said turn, the Deputy turned on his overhead flashing red, blue and white lights.

MM continued into the driveway and parked her car. The Deputy stopped behind her with his lights still flashing. She was in her driveway, parked, keys in hand as she shut her door to see behind her the Deputy getting out of his flashing SUV. He told her to stop, stand where she was and to not move. She complied, and said to the Deputy, "I am home, this is where I live, why am I being stopped"? "So, you live here, in this house"? the Deputy asked, and she replied, "Yes, these are my keys".

The Deputy thought for a moment, then asked her, "Do you know why I stopped you "?

"No", she replied, and the Deputy continued, "You have a lightbulb not working on your license plate. There are two on your car and one is not functioning".

"A lightbulb, that is why you stopped me", more a statement than a question, MM said to the Deputy. "Yes, that is why I stopped you, since this is where you live, I am not going to give you a ticket, just make sure you get it fixed soon". MM said she would get the bulb replaced the next day and asked if she could go, to which the Deputy said have a nice night and went to get back in his vehicle.

His overhead lights turned off and he sped away from the house. MM was shaking and did her best to open the door to her house.

Is this really happening...

A quiet, reserved man who has fought on foreign soil (Fallujah, Iraq, as a Marine) for these United States, had left Vanderbilt Beach and was going to a restaurant on US 41 in the 34108. He was with his wife of ten years plus, and both were looking forward a late dinner, listen to a local music star and share a dance or two. While driving on north on Vanderbilt Drive, the couple saw two CCSO patrol cars headed south one behind the other, they drove passed and both perform immediate U-turns on Vanderbilt and proceeded to catch up and follow them. The patrol cars were no more than two car lengths behind the Marine's pick-up truck, and he wondered aloud to his wife why they were doing so. The couple proceeded to 100th avenue and took a right onto it. The CCSO Deputies also turned right onto 100th avenue, behind the veteran.

Now the patrol cars numbered three and turned on their gleaming red, blue and intimidating white lights. As law abiding citizens, the couple, pulled off the street to let the Deputy Sheriffs have the lane at the nearest driveway and parked.

The couple opened the windows in their truck, and they awaited the deputies who had now parked on the street just behind the driveway where the couple had stopped. To their surprise, the three CCSO deputies ran past their vehicle and into a house to the right, the one that the couple had parked on the house's driveway.

The Marine and his wife thought they were being stopped based on all they had heard occur from friends in the 34108. That said, low and behold, the Deputies following them had other thoughts in mind (the people in the house). The point of sharing this story in this book, is to impart

how even a successful veteran of the US Armed

Services can be influenced by the actions of CCSO

Deputies.

Harassment of a Minor...

Sunday the 12th of August 2019 at 8:45pm, my 16-year daughter came in the front door and announced standing directly in front of me, that she and her girlfriend (Brittany) had just been stopped in front of our house by a Collier County Sherriff.

"You didn't see the lights", she asked? I said I had not and was just finishing dinner while watching ESPN.

"Dad, I got stopped for the plastic lens that covers the license plate on my car!

The Deputy Sherriff said it was illegal to have the lens cover over top the license plate". She continued, "I did not get a ticket, though I did get a warning. The sheriff had been following me, right on my bumper from Walmart". The Walmart is one mile away from our house.

"Was there a reason why he followed you so closely, were you speeding or not using turn signals"? I asked her. "No Dad, I did everything right" and since she had not had a ticket or accident, I assumed she was not lying to me.

Her car has a computer that you can check

average speed, time driving, and fuel used, which I

did weekly while getting gas for her. Her average

speed always was less than 21 miles per hour.

"Dad, he asked me if I had marijuana in the

car and said he could get the dog out of his car to

sniff around mine. He even asked if you or Mom

smoked marijuana".

My daughter then said to the Deputy, "no,

and my Mom is dead".

As she told me this addition to her story, she stood in our living room with her friend, now with tears in her eyes, obviously being reminded of her own loss, nine years past.

Hearing all this, I looked at her and asked, "Are you alright", to which she said yes and went to her room with her friend, shutting the door, saddened. I sat there and thought about what she has just been through.

The more I thought about her experience, the angrier I became, at myself more than anything.

I got up from the couch and went outside. There I walked to the end of the street and stood, gathering my composure.

The street we live on intersects with an arterial avenue through the neighborhood. There was traffic coming from each direction, a few cars at a time. While standing there, I saw a set of lights slow down as it reached my street. Since it was past 9:00pm, and our street is not well illuminated, hence I could not identify the vehicle. Why they slowed down did not make any sense to me, there are no stop signs for the arterial they were on.

The vehicle was a white Ford SUV, painted in Collier County Sheriff graphics of green and gold. It slowed to the intersection then took a left in front of me. It drove on to the end of that street and turned left again. I waited, feeling that he or she would return.

A few minutes went by and another set of lights came to a stop on my left, the next street down. It was the same SUV I had just seen.

It sat at the stop sign for a few minutes, long enough to notice.

No turn signal was used as the Deputy turned right, away from me and proceeded to the exit of the neighborhood.

I turned and began walking back home when I realized why I was angry. I was because most likely the Deputy Sheriff had used "Probable Cause" to pull my daughter over. Did the Deputy Sheriff, "run" the license plate of my daughter's car, where he would find out I was the owner?

Yes, it is legal to research the license plate records of a Collier County citizen, even *if there was no "cause" to do so.*

If, the Deputy Sheriff ran my plates, he realized that I had been convicted of a DUI in 2016. "He had to have asked himself that if he had not seen my daughter and friend get into the car, that was it actually I driving, a possible opportunity for a, "Probable Cause" event"?

I said aloud while walking down the street. *If* he thought it was me driving, is that why he followed so close behind my daughter while he tried to think of a "Probable Cause" to use to justify stopping the car?

Well he found one, the shaded plastic license plate. Below are two lens plate covers, neither from our vehicles. Are these legal?

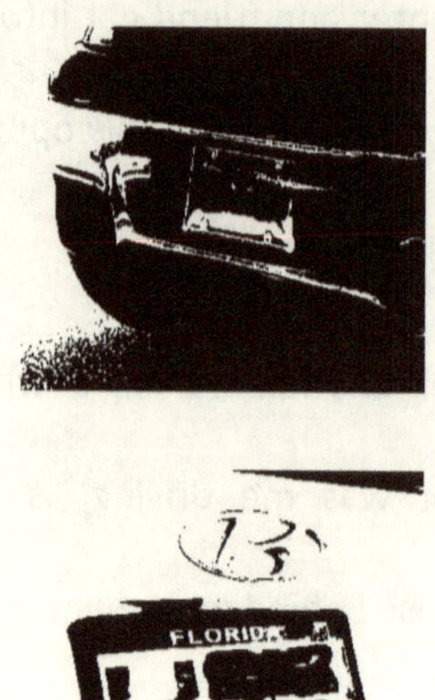

If so then, just how shaded can a license plate lens be?

As you read in the next example of "Probable Cause", you will see where it extends its claws into the Collier County Jail, where local county citizens have been apprehended as potential, "violators" of county or state laws.

Since they have not been, "tried as yet", in custody awaiting bond, they are supposed to be considered as innocent though as you will read in the following pages, may still be subjected to hostility by the Sherriff's Deputies and LEO's the county employs.

Those of you in law enforcement, who choose to treat normal law-abiding citizens with disrespect, should be embarrassed at the lack of humanity you share with the people who pay your salary, benefits and lifestyle you enjoy in Collier County.

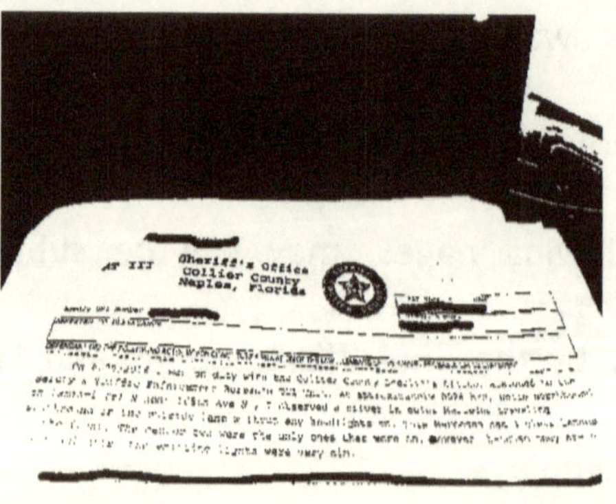

Somethings are personal...

"Thank you, Susan," I said to the bartender as she stapled the top of the brown paper sack that had the remaining wine from the night. "Thank you too", she said.

The jazz was good that evening and the dancing even better. "Enjoyable", I thought while walking out to my two-month-old Mercedes. Turn the key and the automatic lights shone brightly on the parking lot. It was 11:35pm.

I proceeded to the exit of the Pavilion parking lot stopped, then turned right on to

Vanderbilt Beach road, and continued to the first U-turn. Made a legal U-turn near the north Naples sub-station of the Collier County Sheriff and drove east back to US41.

The traffic light was red, changed to green, and I continued with a left turn onto north US41. I needed gas and felt the urge for a coffee and donut from a franchised pastry shop, which was less than one point one (1.1) miles.

The north and south bound lights on US 41 were as bright as can be emitting forty thousand lumens turning the road from night into day.

The traffic signal lights that night was all green, as I made my way to Immokalee Road to make another U turn south to the 7-11 for gas. After filling up, I pulled out southbound again to go to the donut shop. It was closed, but hunger still nagged away in my stomach. A restaurant that was open twenty-four hours a day was a half mile away, so I proceeded to drive to there, though before reaching it, decided against eating fast food and turned right onto 100th Avenue to go to my house on 107th in the Park.

As I made my turn onto 100th Avenue, I looked in the mirror as the lights from another vehicle that had turned behind me burst into my car, illuminating it like the sun in daytime.

They were the red, blue, and white lights of a CCSO patrol car, and I heard the siren. Since there was only me on the road, I steered the Mercedes over to the right, and tapped the button to roll down the driver's window.

"Do you know why I stopped you", the Deputy asked while flashing a bright light in my eyes.

I responded "maybe, the lights"? The Deputy quickly stated, "it was my lights, and they were not illuminated".

I looked over the dash and saw the whole street was lighted from my car including the illumination from the fog lamps.

I had my lights set to automatic and guessed when I got gasoline at the convenience store, they must have reset to a lower illumination, since the convenience store had very bright lights in their parking lot.

When I exited the convenience store, the officer must have seen my car then with two lights yet to re-adjust the four lamps of illumination of US41 there about at 105th Avenue.

When I pulled onto 100th Avenue in Naples Park, my lights adjusted to the darkness, thus having all six lights illuminated versus two. That was why I responded, "maybe" to answer the first question the Deputy Sherriff asked me.

The Deputy asked for my driver's license, registration, and insurance card to which I was, "slow" to respond/find.

I truly was in shock at being, "pulled over" since I had not been so for any type of traffic offense in the past ten years.

Additionally, I had just bought the car I was driving two months earlier, after driving my previous vehicle an SUV for eight years.

Naturally, I was slow to retrieve the documents and he commented about that as a reason to assume I had been drinking that evening.

To which he then asked, "have you been drinking tonight"? I did not answer, and he asked again. I mumbled, "yes" and told him where. He left to go back to his vehicle, one of those unmarked (Ghost) sedan type of Ford.

In the arrest report, the CCSO's Deputy Sherriff and Patrol Officer, assigned to Safety and Traffic Enforcement Bureau's DUI Unit, stated the following:

At 12:26am (0026 hours) while he traveled northbound on Tamiami Trail N near 105th Ave. N, "I observed a silver Mercedes traveling southbound in the outside lane without headlights on".

In the next sentence he states, "This Mercedes had 4 clear lenses in the front".

The Officer's next statement was, "The vehicle then turned south onto 100th Ave. in Naples Park. After the vehicle turned into the park, I noticed that the emitting lights were a lot brighter than before".

So, the Deputy Sherriff first stated no lights were on and in the next sentence stated that one set of lights was "on". Furthermore, he commented that the "lights were clear", how did he know this if they were not on?

For clarity, the, "Florida State Statutes" about the lighting of a two-axle motor vehicle (an automobile) is as follows:

Title XXIII, Chapter 316, Motor vehicles, State Uniform Traffic Control –

(1)   Every motor vehicle shall be equipped with at least two headlamps with at least one on each side of the front of the motor vehicle, which headlamps shall comply with the requirements and limitations set forth in this chapter and shall show a white light.

316.237   Multiple-beam/road-lighting/equipment.

(1)   Except as hereinafter provided, *the headlamps or the auxiliary driving lamp or the auxiliary passing lamp or combination thereof on motor vehicles shall be so arranged that the driver may select at will between distributions of light projected to different elevations and such lamps may, __in addition, be so__*

<u>*arranged that such selection can be made*</u>

<u>*automatically*</u>.

316.239 Single-beam road-lighting equipment

Are allowed if the single distribution of light

complies with the following requirements and

limitations:

(a)   The headlamps shall be so aimed that when

the vehicle is not loaded none of the high intensity

portion of the light shall, at a distance of 25 feet

ahead, project higher than a level of five inches

below the level of the center of the lamp from which

it comes, and in no case higher than 42 inches above

the level on which the vehicle stands at a distance of

75 feet ahead.

(b)   The intensity shall be enough to reveal persons and vehicles at a distance of at least 200 feet.

For consideration – Both my vehicle and the Deputy Sheriff's patrol car were traveling towards each other at approximately 45 miles per hour (the posted speed limit). At 45 miles per hour, a vehicle travels 66 feet or 22 yards PER SECOND.

THOUSAND ONE, THOUSAND TWO, THOUSAND THREE, in three seconds each vehicle traveled 198 feet or over half the length of a football field (well within the requirements of Title XXIII, Chapter 316, 1, 316.237, and 316.239).

How was it possible in that short period for the Deputy Sheriff to have enough time to check the "clarity" of the of my vehicle's FOUR headlight lenses UNLESS THE LIGHTS WERE ON AND PRODUCING SUFFICIENT ILLUMINATION?

In the *2004, Mercedes C240 Owner's Manual* statements about the ***front lights when in automatic position they adjust their brightness to the outside ambient level of light*** (such as on US 41 and when turning onto 100th Ave).

Other Comments on the Arrest Report...

The Deputy stated that my eyes were, "glassy". I take daily prescription medicine related to heart disease (blood pressure & anxiety). Those are one of the side effects. The Deputy did not ask if was taking any medications.

The Deputy stated that when I stepped out of the vehicle, he noticed me stumble as I walked to the rear of his vehicle. I had on worn-out two-and-a-half-year-old flip flops.

The Deputy stated that he felt he had probable cause to arrest me of a DUI and placed me in the patrol car.

At no time, was I read or made aware of my Miranda Rights or Warnings (right to remain silent, that anything you say may be used against you, and that you have the right to an attorney, if you cannot afford one will be provided to you).

Failure to issue the Miranda warning renders evidence so obtained to not be admissible in the court.

The warning became a national police requirement when ordered by the US Supreme Court in the 1966 case Miranda v. Arizona.

Important Timeline –

12:26am, the Officer sees me driving south on US41.

12:39am, the Officer arrests and places me in the patrol car.

13 minutes had passed and how can the questions be asked, responded to, and evaluated in just 13 minutes?

Furthermore, the Deputy made no remarks about how my vehicle was being driven (was not swerving, was not speeding, or was not driving aggressively and did use turn signals).

My DUI arrest by the Collier County Deputy Sheriff was **based on probable cause and he had used this tactic in almost a third (27.8%) of his arrests from June 2015 through June 2016.**

The Deputy Sheriff also administered the Breathalyzer to me at the Collier County Jail Processing Center.

Should this protocol demand a second LEO (Law Enforcement Officer) conduct and evaluate the test?

Duty of Booking Officer. In addition to any other duty, the officer who commits a defendant to custody has the following duties:

(1) The officer shall immediately advise the defendant:

(A) Of the right to counsel.

(B) That, if the defendant is unable to pay a lawyer, one will be provided immediately at no charge.

(2) If the defendant requests counsel or advises the officer that he or she cannot afford counsel, the officer shall immediately and effectively place the defendant in communication with the (office of) public defender of the circuit in which the arrest was made.

Holding Area – Collier County Jail Center

The, "Holding Area" is directly after you have been frisked in the entryway, "Sally Port", of locking doors from the garage where you are first brought, when placed under arrest in Collier County. There are plenty of plastic chairs, telephones, a ring of holding cells, concrete and cold, brightly lighted with a drain in the middle to wash away, "throw-up" and bodily fluids including blood when necessary.

From an elevated perch, watching you always, were five to six LEO's (Law Enforcement Officers) of various sizes, genders, and races.

All the LEO's were wearing standard and what appeared to be not so standard weapons (handguns).

The LEO's are your first encounter screaming at you to, "stand up, sit down, shut up and listen to me", all you will become accustomed to hearing.

I was allowed one call, to which I notified my sister in Ft. Myers of the situation. In less than an hour's time (3:30am), she very kindly arrived with $1,000 bond to gain my release; the jail staff would not accept the bail amount and process documents. Why?

With the bond not accepted, she then left the County Jail in Naples, drove back to her home in Ft. Myers, FL. She would return to the Jail Center, three additional times at 6:30am, 9:30am and finally at 2:30pm after having to post a now $3,000 bond as determined by the weekend Judge. Evidently, I did not qualify for the standard $1,000 DUI bond amount.

At 07:30am, prior to being taken into the cell blocks of the county jail, you see a nurse for evaluation.

The nurse checking me said, "Everybody in Collier County goes to jail, I see them all from eight (8) years old to ninety-eight (98), yeah, isn't that a shame, they take in a 98-year-old? There ought to be a limit on age, don't you agree"?

From there it was down the hall, escorted by a LEO to receive a full body x-ray like one received at an airport. The LEO operating the x-ray machine thought it was quite funny and let everyone know standing nearby that he could see I had a vasectomy.

Wonder what he thought of my circumcision?

After that it was back down the hall to receive new clothes, a green jumpsuit, and a dingy white pair of crocs. No socks, you do not deserve those. You are then lined up in front of two restrooms to change into your new duds and receive your naked body strip search in one of the restrooms. Yes, you do have to turn, touch your toes and then spread your cheeks for the visual inspection of your ass to be followed by lifting your testicles so the two officers in the same restroom can have a "visual" on that area of your body.

"Freshly" changed into your new attire, you deposit whatever you had in your pockets and clothes into a paper sack to be stapled and given to a county worker to deposit in an adjoining room.

"LINE UP, AGAINST THE WALL", two LEO's command and demand. You then walk to where you will receive a bag of toiletries, a sheet, thin blanket and what can be called as the most useless pillow you can imagine.

On to CELLBLOCK C. Another, "Sally Port or Man Trap" with a clear glass visual of your fellow inmates, cells, tables bolted to the floor and a row of telephones on the nearest wall. You receive your cell number and if lucky no one else will as well, so you do not have to decide who will be sleeping on the top bunk with a fluorescent light beaming above you all night. I did not have a, "roommate" for the evening, made my bed and laid down as the electronic cell door closed.

Sleep.

There is a toilet in the cell, though the view of the outside in the cell block is all inmates and tattoos. In the morning, the LEO's brought ice water in an orange fifty-gallon container along with plastic cups. The inmates line up to get a glass and I to this day, nothing has tasted so good. Appreciate the little things.

Food served, let us just say it is not fit for human consumption, with exception to an orange, a boiled egg, cereal, and a small carton of milk you can open yourself.

If you try to make a call, all must be with a charge to the receiver of such and a notification, "You are receiving a call from a Collier County Inmate at the Collier County Jail".

Inmates are what you expect, the usual characters.

Other than the overweight ones, they are like what you see at a convenience store, Skinny, like all they have eaten was white bread and bologna sandwiches in their life. Short, quarter inch blond hair, buzz cut and a boxed pack of Marlboros in their hip pocket.

Or maybe they are as bald as a white supremacist from Northern Idaho hinterlands. Many I encountered had limited education and possibly quit high school in 10th grade.

There is a lot of red tan, mustached or goatee wearing types too, that you can just guess drive new Camaros or Mustangs, with blacked out tinted windows like they did in their teens, though now are fifty-five or more in years of age.

If you want to talk with your jail LEO's, "keepers" it must be done through a hole in the wall the size of a cement brick of concrete.

First night turns into morning, 730am, and two hours before 1st appearances at 9:30am. Then the LEO's line us up in the hallway, just outside the cell block.

"Right side only, hands behind your back, walk in a straight line and don't speak" they say. The LEO's escort us, beside behind, and just in front.

One LEO speaks to what looks like an 18-year old boy, an inmate behind me, walking with his brother no less, "Two for One", said the LEO, to the youngest brother.

He mumbled something under his breath, the LEO picked up on it and yelled, "What'd you say, what'd you say punk", in his best northeast US accent. No response from the kid, his brother said in a hushed voice, "shut up" at his sibling. The LEO continued calling the kid a "punk", with what had to be spit rolling off his tongue, "Junior, what you got a problem, you got one with me"?

Before the final vowel was formed and enunciated by the LEO, I heard a body slam into the wall and turned around with the other inmates to see the kid hit the ground with the LEO kicking and punching him as he fell.

Another LEO bellowed above the noise caused by the altercation, "Straighten up, all of you", we were told, "face forward and walk".

We did as were told as one LEO after another ran past us, each taking a punch into the kid or bouncing him against the wall. Blood splattered everywhere.

I saw one LEO, all three hundred (300) pounds of himself trying to run with a fellow comrade, laughing and making a joke of his fat buddy's effort to join into the ambush. We did not see the almost juvenile again that day, they took him somewhere.

As directed, we continued our walk to a jail conference room where we would make the first appearance before the judge on TV. The public defender assigned to us, said we would all get to speak with him prior to being in front of the judge that Saturday morning.

There would be the sixteen (16) inmates

before my name was called to meet the Public

Defender, so I did not get to speak with him nor did

the remaining twelve (12) temporary residents of

cell block C.

What did that lack of counsel mean to me

and my case? The anticipated bond sum of $1,000

grew to $3,000 when the judge saw me standing for

the camera.

—————————————————————————

Bond Process...

As said before, my sister arrives at 2:30pm with now $3,000 bond it was her fourth trip in twelve hours (Ft. Myers to Naples at 3:30am, 6:30am and 9:30am).

Her and I left the jail, picked up my car, hotter than hell outside (95+ degrees), paid $320 bucks, found the Deputy Sheriff left parting gifts for me including the yellow tape in my car that I had to walk the line with, and the 1/8 bottle of wine left on the floor in a sack that he did not find. Dinner with

daughter, home by 7:00pm

____

Monday (06.27.2016)

Went to the Collier County courthouse to receive paperwork about the ticket and case.

None would be available until Wednesday morning (with 6 days remaining on an unsuspended license). Cost $17 for the records was told I could drive for 10 days. Took eight (8) hours personal time from work. Cost $216.

Wednesday (06.29.2016)

Was turned down for a public attorney by the Clerk of Courts.

Applied for a public attorney with the judge of my case.   A private attorney's cost was $3,500.

Thursday (06.30.2016)

Was approved for a "hardship" license. Cost $25. Signed up for DUI School. Cost $267. Received "hardship" license. Cost $207.

Wednesday (07.06.2016)

Was told I would need to go in front of the judge in a "hearing format" to plead my case for a public attorney. Decided to represent myself.

Arraignment (07.20.2016)

I was awoken the at morning at 6:45am by a Deputy Collier County Sheriff banging on my front door. He stated to me that there had been a 911 call originating from my address. I showed him my cell which had no such call being made and told him there was no one else in the house (my daughter was with friends/sleepover). Was this harassment or a friendly wake-up visit?

8:30am, Collier County Courthouse, Courtroom B2

Full house, me the only one with a suit (black, light blue shirt, blue Hermes tie) other than the lawyers. Sat down, bench style, just like in a church without the kneeling step.

90% of the ninety defenders there to make their first plea were under 40 years of age. **85% were Hispanic or Latino in a county where just 28% of the population is.**

One attorney is an interpreter, a fellow worker bee for Collier County that I would ride the elevator in the parking garage some mornings with, made a double take when he saw me.

The Judge, in his 60's, big guy, dressed in a light fishing shirt common the Collier County boat owners, full beard and balding explained the process in English and Spanish (he was born in Mexico, though was of US parents). He was patient, had a good smile and was friendly.

I wondered how my next Judge would be, the one that would decide my fate and punishment.

One defendant started shouting because he wanted his case to be heard soon, "Come on man", he roared and continued, "like being shot with a Walmart bullet", he fell to the ground and "Praise Jesus", just like he had been, "saved" at a religious function.

I was called to the front of the court where two Florida State Attorneys sat at a non-descript wooden desk and accepted pleas. They also offered if you plead guilty or no contest, a sentence.

I received a, **"first offer"**, it is on the next page.

Fine	$1,000
Court Costs	$500
DUI Class	$267
Substance Abuse Evaluation	$405
Community Service, (50 hours)	$500
Probation of One Year	$670
Ignition Lock, 6 Months	$575
Substance Evaluations	$300
Random Drug and Alcohol Testing	$360
Impoundment of Vehicle Ten Days	$300
Reinstatement of Driver's License	$100
Sub-Total	**$4,977**
Added to what I had spent:	
Bond posted, June 25th	$300
Vehicle retrieved June 25th	$320
Records retrieved June 29th	$17
Administrative Hearing (Hardship D|	$25
Received "Hardship DL" July 1st	$207
Sub-Total	**$869**
A Grand Total (so far)	**$6,041**

Trials...

Defending Yourself, a Quick Tutorial

So, you want to defend yourself?!   Then get

acquainted with this important rule.

Demand for Discovery

Florida Rule 3.220. Discovery,

(b) Prosecutor's Discovery Obligation.

(1) Within 15 days after service of the Notice

of Discovery, the prosecutor shall serve a written

Discovery Exhibit which shall disclose to the

defendant and permit the defendant to inspect,

copy, test, and photograph the following information and material within the state's possession or control.

Information was not provided, and I (the defendant) filed a Motion to Dismiss Case on August 9, 2016.

Filed Motion to Dismiss was due to 15 days had passed since the Demand for Discovery was filed per Florida Rule 3.220, Prosecutor's Obligation to comply to request.

Went to District Attorney's office (Courthouse) to attempt retrieval of state's evidence. Submitted exhibits/evidence for Pre-Trial to Clerk of Courts & Assistant District Attorney (ADA).

Received response from State for Demand for Discovery (8 days past the deadline from them to me).

Requested video evidence or written statements about if Miranda Rights (rights of the accused) were provided.

Interview with Substance Abuse Evaluator –
made to go to 12 weeks of 1-hour counseling
sessions. Submitted exhibits/evidence for Pre-Trial
to Clerk of Courts & ADA.

Filed Motion to Suppress Dash cam and
inside vehicle video evidence due to 5th Amendment
Rights of Self Incrimination filed.

Filed Motion to Dismiss due to failure to
provide Breathalyzer certificate information from
07.26.16 request and failure to provide information
from Demand for Discovery of Video or Requested
Written evidence of Miranda Rights/ Rights of the

Accused being given to Defendant, — none was provided.

July 27 through July 29, 2016

— Attended DUI School

August 09

— Requested through CCSO Public Records Request, a Demand for Discovery of the dash cam pictures, video of the arrest, jail video and any written or confiscated information or records. Was denied access to pictures and arrest video (was sent through ADA).

August 12

– Received jail video and 911 audio, from the early morning wake-up call from the Deputy Sherriff on my day of Arraignment (6:07am call, music, no words spoken).

August 15

– Went to District Attorney's office (Courthouse) to attempt retrieval of state's evidence.

August 17

– Received response from State for Demand for Discovery (8 days past the deadline). They did not care.

August 22

– Requested video evidence or written statements about whether Miranda Rights (rights of the accused) were provided.

August 26

– Submitted exhibits/evidence for Pre-Trial to Clerk of Courts & ADA.

August 29

– Filed Motion to Suppress Dash cam and inside vehicle video evidence due to 5th Amendment Rights of Self Incrimination filed.

Serious dreams of suicide.

August 30

– Interview with Collier County Counseling.

Ordered to attend twelve (12) group counseling sessions. Ordered to attend four (4) AA meetings.

September 08, 2016 – Pre-Trial 1

Driver's License suspension at that time was 76 days. Offer was to continue suspension until one year was completed. DUI School and evaluation completed. Attended Collier County Counseling's evaluation.

$1,238 spent so far, (plus 3 vacation days for $896).

Pre-Trial (2), December 16th, 2016

six (6) months since arrest...

First, the players (court reporters, private attorneys, interpreters, etc.) all take their places and await the Judge to enter the Chambers. There were three Sherriff's Deputies including the one arresting me, a Public Defender, an Assistant District Attorney, and other support officials. None of the public was attending.

I pleaded my case to the Judge and was well represented by the Public Defender.

The Judge agreed to take all the evidence I had presented home for review and that we would reconvene in two days-time.

I felt as though, I had a chance to defeat this probable cause event and went home pleased.

Two days later, the Judged ruled and I was Adjudged Guilty. I accepted the conditions which now did not include my car being disabled for ten days. Everything else remained the same (one year probation that may be discontinued after six months with all other conditions completed, six months driver's license suspension, six months interlock where you must provide a sample of your breath to start your car, fifty hours community service or $500, a $1,500 fine including court costs (prosecutor, defense attorney, court), increased car insurance though not part of the penalties, classes and counseling.

I was told by my Public Defender to report immediately to the Probation Office and schedule my orientation. It was on the first floor of the Courthouse.

Upon arriving where Probation offices in the Collier County Courthouse were located, I found everyone was at lunch, so the actual Director of Probation was manning the front counter. I told him what I had been told as to reporting and he decided to perform my orientation himself. Maybe he saw my County Badge, maybe not, though that said it was kind for him to personally explain everything and provide all the forms I would need. So far, he was the best person I had encountered and I for one appreciate his thoughtfulness. I felt like a human

being as I left the Courthouse that day.

Counseling

DUI School, twelve (12) hours total over three consecutive days, beginning at 6:00pm.

Mr. Z, a late thirty (30) something probation officer teaches the class, tall, overweight, glasses, dark brown eyes, and a Patriots fan.

The first night, raining, located in East Naples in a non-descript two story building with a suite for the class and one for "Intake" into the Florida State Corrections (prior to being sent to State Prison). Additionally, the building is directly across the street from where I worked in the Government Center.

There were fourteen (14) of us in the class, 55% were men, 45% were women, all ages from their 20's, 30's, 40's, two 55-year old's and a 77-year-old with just two demographics represented, 80% white and 20% Hispanic or Latino.

The classroom 28' by 16', smell was musty, old dirty carpet, 75 degrees (outside is 90+ at 6:00pm), three rows with three desks to a row, no windows, and a tile ceiling.

Fellow students carried the scents of construction work sweat, cigarettes and perfume.

The class decided on the first day that everyone should shower before attending the next day's class.

General group attitude day one: depressed, those 45 years old and above seemed embarrassed, tired, bored (though the young were engaged in the class). Most have tans and lots of tattoos. After the first day, in the remaining days everyone took the same seats as they had sat the previous evening. Wonder what the psychologists would have to say about that?

How we arrived to partake in this form of education, – six (6) had accidents in cars or trucks, six (6) refused to take breathalyzer, all eight (8) of the women received free drinks the night of being stopped, eight (8) were professionals, four (4) in healthcare including an Intensive Care Nurse (ICU), and four (4) were construction workers.

All passed their test and urine analysis (last day) and received their certificates to present to their Probation Officers

.

Counseling Session 1

Up to twelve (12) hours with most taking place at twelve noon one day each week.

Counseling, Evaluation ($45), 12 counseling sessions of 1 hour each at $30 (or $360), must be taken consecutively. Basically, DUI School repeated with open session for "feel good" emotional outpouring.

Counseling Session 2

Another evaluation, and then six (6) weeks of one hour of class each, plus drug/alcohol testing and probable release, a total $321. Basically, DUI

School, Counseling 1, Counseling 2 and more "open

sessions".

Feel like shit, this is never ending. Want to

feel powerless; the drug alcohol counselor can

decide if you will attend six (6) or up to sixteen (16)

sessions, time, and money, then you have

final judgment for release.

The counselors also report everything from

your attitude to participation to the judge and

probation.

Alcoholics Anonymous (AA)

Four (4) hours and guess what, I found out afterward you can take all in one day versus four individual sessions. More crying and very depressing personal stories are shared and conveyed.

Mothers Against Drunk Driving (MADD)

Conducted in the evening, two hours, in one of the County Court's Chambers. For a fee of seventy-five dollars, you receive painful tales, no other way to describe the encounter.

Probation...

Probation, the first seven months consisted of a meeting every four weeks in the County Courthouse with an assigned Probation Officer. Mine was named AB. Since I had complied with all my assigned, "conditions", they very happily took my seventy-five ($75) dollars a month without complications. With everything completed, I petitioned the Court to end my Probation period in October, two months early.

As stated previously, when you are "on probation" in Collier County, for most DUI convictions, you most likely will not be allowed to have alcohol in your residence let alone in your body.   I got the first command correct, though missed listening, reading, or obliging the second.

VOP

(Violation of Probation)

Almost one year and a month from my arrest for the DUI in Naples Park, while still on probation with a request to discontinue it with six months past, I incurred the following.

It had been a good day at work. Had spent the afternoon on location, shooting interviews with local Collier County citizens for an, "Affordable Housing" public service video for the Community and Housing Services Division of Public Services. All had been prepared at a Fleischman park with the late July weather being as perfect as one could ask for. Upon completion, I went with the film crew to enjoy a beer in downtown Naples.

Afterward, I drove home to find a Deputy Sherriff's patrol car parked on my neighbor's driveway.

When I pulled onto my driveway, the Sherriff did the same, immediately exited his car as well with a Probation Officer. Hence would begin the "official house visit". My daughter was not home, so I welcomed both into our house.

There, they checked my refrigerator for alcohol products and trash. None were found.

The Probation Officer opened a small box he had with him and told me he needed a breath sample to complete the visit.

I had consumed the one beer, forty-five minutes earlier and did not think there would be anything left in my system that would Identify such. I was wrong, had a trace of alcohol in my breath, and before I could respond, my hands were behind my back in handcuffs.

"A bump in the road", did he really say that to me about my situation? While my face is smashed against the full yellow plastic divider separating, 'him" the Senior Probation Officer and a County Deputy Sheriff (them) from me in the patrol car.

My arms tied, aching, searing with 56 years'

worth of pain? Why is this form of treatment

necessary?

The next day Violation of Probation arrest

report contained the incorrect original judge listed

on the form the Senior Probation Officer used to

recommend the Judge that I serve the next ten (10)

days in a row, before going to Probation Court to be

judged again. So much for the, "Bump in the road"

comment he made the day before. He knew I had

a minor child and would need to decide for her care.

The Judge did not accept the Senior Probation Officer's recommendation, reduced it to eight days for time served, weekends only and I would be released that day to return a week later to begin punishment.

I left the court, once again temporarily a free person. I again saw the, "Senior Probation Officer" during Hurricane Irma cruising in his dark blue Ford police sedan on US41 making a U-turn. His passenger window was down, he saw me, and I saw him.

Third time while I was still on probation, was on a Sunday, lunch time, when he turned off Immokalee Road into a shopping center where I was walking my dog and having a morning coffee. He was driving fast, not using turn signals, pulled up to a taqueria, but did not get out of the car. He just sat there, watching me and me watching him. Guess he did not have a, "Probable Cause" event to pursue me with.

____

Violation of Probation (VOP) – Weekly Jail Time

Friday afternoon, 5:00pm leaving work...

In my case, this meant walking from one government building to the Collier County Jail's front entrance. There I would find other poor souls waiting on blue plastic chairs to begin their weekend of confinement. It would begin the next four Friday's in a row at exactly 6:00pm and not end until Sunday evening at 6:00pm.

Once inside the County Jail, first was entry through the, "Sally Port" into the Holding Area (Collier County Jail Center), but first, you are place against the wall, told to raise your hands above your head and empty your pockets (if you had not already done so outside into a set of lockers provided for such). The whole process of going from office business clothes to a green inmate jumpsuit, must be designed to remind you have gone from independence to dependence and willful submittal to humiliation.

I am a heart patient, which means I require medicines daily to continue to walk on this planet. Even though, the Jail staff had my medicine requirements and schedule, the prescriptions somehow did not arrive the first weekend, leaving me open to a third heart attack possibility, a stroke, or better yet a mental breakdown.

You sit in the, "Holding Area", along with the other soon to be inmates, on green plastic chairs and do not speak. If you do speak, you will be greeted with a stern look and most likely be told to, "Shut Up".

You wait your turn with the County Nurse to discuss your medicine situation, and perform all the normal tests, blood pressure, heart rate and weight readings.

You might be told to provide a breath sample to check for alcohol.

When a group of four to six have seen the Nurse, You then get marched to collect your green jumpsuit and "Crocs" and place your clothes into a paper sack. This is done in one of two restrooms where with two LEO's, you will get stripped searched.

"Lift your testicles again, cough, using your hands, spread your ass cheeks and cough again". I had this happen on each of my four weekends as a two-hundred and twenty-five dollar a night resident of the Collier County Jail. On the third weekend strip search, a LEO retained my blue checkered boxers, while I stood there naked.

When I asked him why I was not given my shorts back, he replied, "you don't get them back, not if I do the search".

Sunday afternoon, and 6:00pm does not come fast enough. It was August and Southwest Florida heat was oppressive.

Fourteen hours pass for me to go from Sunday at 6:00pm, an Inmate in the Collier County Jail to an employee of the Collier County Board of Commissioners at 8:00am, Monday morning.

My boss's boss asks me at our weekly planning meeting, "how was your weekend"?

To which I responded, "It was ok, was served

food not for human consumption, slept on a metal

shelf attached to a brick wall, did not look anyone of

authority in the eyes, was yelled at collectively with

the other inmates for not sitting four to a table for

breakfast at 4:30am, lunch, dinner or for speaking to

each other. My entertainment consisting of other

inmates singing of hymns, inmates screaming at

midnight just to wake others up, relieving myself in

a toilet by the cell door, open to everyone's view and

for 48 hours not being able to speak with my 15 year

old daughter. Yeah boss it was a great weekend, thanks for asking".

My first weekend, I met a Mercedes salesman, an Air Conditioner Repairman, a Construction Worker and with me, we formed a loose band of brothers. We all served the same jail terms as, "Weekenders".

In jail, I learned to think of time in different increments, such as 120 months sounds better than 10 years.

I learned new barter skills, such as trading food for boxer shorts, bread for cookies, and to always be aware that felons await the weekenders to arrive. Extra entertainment for them. Additionally, when I received my first envelope back from the, "Jailer's" who store your clothes, I was missing $11 dollars. I was told that is called an, "admission fee" and to not bring cash in the future.

The second weekend I met a fellow named Chris and told him that I ever wrote a book about this experience, I would share his story.

Chris, thirty-five years old, a father of five children and a grandfather of one. He showed me a scar and told this quick story. While in custody once, he slit his forearm up the middle like filleting a fish. He did this, so he could be taken out of the Collier Jail and let into a hospital to recover. He did not say much after that, though wanted to share.

____

Justice

Targeting, Racism and Class Distinction...

The sworn duty of the Collier County Sheriff's Office is to ***preserve and protect the lives, property, and constitutional guarantees of all persons***.

What we see:

Is this not a problem?

In Collier County, the 1% - always in the lead,

safe to stay near home (Port Royal), safe from racial

differences and the County Deputy Sheriffs.

The farm worker (with no real discretionary income), with a DUI are stuck in the system due to the fines.

The hospitality worker has no upward mobility because with a DUI, they cannot get a promotion or a new job in a different field.

The construction worker with a DUI, keeps them on the job site, forever tied to hammers and saws.

In Immokalee, which make up 35% of the DUI arrests, it is 90% Hispanic with the lowest family income as compared to the rest of Collier County.

Naples Manor shares up to 20% of the DUI arrests and is made up of African American, Hispanic, or Latino and lower income Caucasians. Golden Gate Parkway leading to Golden Gate City make up 15% DUI arrests, low and low middle income, African American, Hispanic, or Latino and Caucasians.

What is not to love living in Collier Collier's county...well, included are arrests while **Hurricane Irma** was raging. One such arrest led to "tasering" of an Everglades City resident by an authorized CCSO's, "taser trainer" *in the no less than the county jail...ended in the citizen's death!*

So, is this not a problem?

The Collier County citizens besieged with arrests from a recent 30-day study over the holidays in 2019 into 2020 (DEC 20, 2019 through JAN 20, 2020) yielded the following data. Based on five hundred and twenty-three (523) arrests.

30.4% of arrests (*) were citizens of <u>Hispanic</u> or <u>Latino</u> descent, though they make up **27.2% of the population** (**)! **11.8% more arrests than their percent of the population**?

16.8% percent of arrests (*) were of <u>African American</u> origin, though they make up **6.8% of the population** (**)! **A 147.1% more arrests than their percent of the population**?

52.8% percent of arrests (*) were of Caucasian origination, and they make up 63.6% (**) of the population. A 16.9% reduction in arrests versus their population?

In a CCSO arrest/incarceration study from February and March 2019 yielded 880 arrests (*) and they reconfirm the data from December (2019) and January (2020).

27.9% (*) arrested were of Hispanic or Latino origin, 18.2% (*) were of African American descent and 52.8% (*) were again Caucasians.

In the data from February and March 2019, the areas of the county appear to have more arrest activity than others. They were:

East Naples (zip code-34112) with 9.8% of arrests.

South Naples (zip code-34113) with 6.4% of arrests.

Immokalee (zip code-34142) with 11.5% of arrests.

Over 27.7% of arrests come from three (3) zip codes out of more than twenty (20) in Collier County.

The average household income for the areas (below) are **compared in** red percentages to **Collier Countywide Household Income of $68,300.**

This data provides a classic definition of "intolerance" and divides neighbors and neighborhoods.

East Naples - 34112 $44,432   -53.7%

South Naples - 34113 $48,281   -41.4%

Immokalee (34142) $27,760   -146.1%

(*) The arrests were provided by the daily CCSO online reporting of previous day activity that ended with incarceration. Data includes the zip codes (***) which delineate location in Collier County.

(**) The population figures are from American Fact Finder (AFF), US Census reporting from 2013 through 2017.

 (****) Income data was sourced from American Community Services (ACS), US Census reporting 2019

(*****)   NAHB,News-and-Economics/Housing-Economics/Indices/Housing-Opportunity-Index

From data going back three years, in July and August 2017, there were 833 arrests in the county and they statistics are below:

Golden Gate (34116) had the largest number of arrests at 123 and made up **14.8%** of the total.

The **Airport-Pulling Road (34112)** area was 2nd with 121 arrests or **14.5%** of the total.

Immokalee (34142) was 3rd with 118 arrests, or **14.2%** of the total.

They were **followed by**:

South Naples (34113), 65 arrests **(7.8%)**.

Fairgrounds (34120), 61 arrests **(7.3%)**.

Goodlette Frank Road (34104), 51 arrests

(6.1%).

Naples Park (34108), 46 arrests (**5.5%)**.

Is there targeting of Naples Park for DUI arrests?

Ask yourself this, how is it statistically possible that there would be three citizens of one small section of Collier County, to be stopped for a "Probable Cause" event and then each arrested for a DUI, all in just days from each other? How also, is it possible for at any given time, there are at least five (5) tax paying Citizens on County Probation that live in Naples Park? It is not possible, unless the CCSO is targeting that neighborhood.

How can that statement be true? Just the facts, I present. I have had thirty-eight (38) neighbors from Naples Park from 2016 through 2019 arrested in the Park on all sorts of charges, most though from a "DUI" that originated with a stop for, "Probable Cause".

Friends, hard-working people in Naples Park, my neighborhood have fallen victim to the predatory practice (Probable Cause) by a County Deputy. Think I am bullshitting you, look at these names (though just initials):

JG, JP, LL, JR, PG, BC, MM, BL, ZL, CL, AR, SB, SN, DS, MB, KM, MM, MM, JM, JR, PB, BK, MH, TD, AS, PE, TD, JS, CV, AA, BD, SY, VM, RR, ER, NZ, SK, HR, thirty eight (38) Collier County Citizens of Naples Park.

Collier County Curfew Due to Hurricane Irma...

A County-wide curfew was set due to Hurricane Irma. Based on what you have read so far, it is not difficult to imagine CCSO's Deputy Sheriffs foaming at the mouth to use the 9:00pm "Hurricane Curfew" as another form of "Probable Cause", leading to an arrest.

In one day tracked, Sunday, September 17, 2017 there were thirty-four (34) arrests. Sixteen (16) or 47.1% included a charge for violating curfew (VIOLATION OF DISASTER REPAREDNESS

EMERGENCY MANAGEMENT PROCAMATION).

Bonds ranged from $1,000 to $2,000.

Curfew was discontinued at 2:30pm on Monday, Sept. 18, 2017.

February 10, 2020 –

Last night, while driving a one-mile trip from Trader Joe's to my house, I was followed by one of the Collier County Deputy Sheriffs. From US 41, south to 106th avenue, through three stop signs (8th, 7th and 107th), three turns with the last turn into my driveway. Why did he follow me? Fear and intimidation, maybe?

DOLLARS (It is about the Money)

The following two (2) pages contains a recap of what my, "Probable Cause" event cost without the use of a private attorney. I had the excellent services of a Public Defender. Thank You Sir!

Towing of my car	$320
Bond	$300
Driver's License Record	$17
DUI School	$267
Hardship License Interview	$25
1st Hardship License	$207
Jail Video	$28
Car Audio	$2
Counseling Evaluation	$45
Counseling 1	$416

MADD Class	$44
Ignition Lock (6 months)	$889
Additional Auto Insurance (3 yrs.)	$6,000
Court Fees	$1,588
Court Fees (misc.)	$50
Probation (10 months)	$750
2nd Hardship License	$107
Urine Testing	$50
Counseling Evaluation 2	$330
Community Service	$500
Driver's License Reinstatement	$65
Cost of time off	$1,512
TOTAL	**$13,512**

This was 1/3 (33%) of my annual take home pay in 2016.

An **Alternative to the Existing System of Prosecuting and Financing DUI Convictions, a fairer Substitute for Consideration Follows –**

Make the fines and related costs proportionate to the individual's income. Not thirty-three percent (33%) of net salary as in my case. Do not penalize the less unfortunate.

A Three – Tiered Approach

Annual taxable individual income of less than $50,000 would have fines and all other related costs to not exceed $3,500 and does not include private legal fees.

Annual taxable individual income of more than $50,000 though less than $100,000 would have fines and all other related costs to not exceed $7,500 and as well does not include private legal fees.

Annual taxable income of more than $100,000 would have fines and all other related costs to not exceed $12,500 and as well does not include private legal fees.

**Collier County's Criminal Misdemeanor System
Benefactors include -**

The CCSO, its Deputies, LEO's, Lawyers, Judges and Administration Serve the Collier County Population in 2019 of 376,500 people.

In 2018, there were 1,391 sheriff employees at a cost of $181,792,000.

In 2018, law enforcement's Deputy Sheriffs numbered 990 and its LEO's numbered 353, in total for a cost of $126,402,700. **One Hundred and Twenty-Six Million Dollars.   Over $94,000 per person cost.**

The arrest Detention Corrections in 2018, posted a $44,002,400. **Forty-Four Million Dollars.**

In 2018, the Clerk of Courts reported the cost of Felonies were $18,400,000, Jury's cost $7,400,000, and the cost for Juveniles were $4,500,000.

On top of those costs to arrest and prosecute Collier County Citizens, please see on this and the following pages the other benefactors of Collier County Legal.

(Please note: 15% of arrests made in Collier County are individuals who do not live in Collier County.)

Probation Officers

Bond Providers

Substance Abuse Providers Evaluations

Southwest Florida Counseling (contractors)

Drug and Alcohol Testing Providers

DUI Evaluator

DUI Schools

Provider of "Hardship" Driver's License Testing

Reinstatement of Driver's License Providers

Internet Mug Shot Communicators

Phone Message Providers ("You are receiving a call

from a Collier County Inmate)

Tow Truck Companies

Private Attorneys

Inmates Food, Clothing, Medical Providers

Vehicle Insurance Providers

MADD (Mothers Against Drunk Driving)

AA (Alcoholics Anonymous)

Ignition Lock Providers

Counselors

____

FOR A DUI IN FLORIDA, YOU RECEIVE AS ADDITIONAL PUNISHMENT WITH A PERMANENT CRIMINAL RECORD

In, "about a half of a second, any interested person, will be able to locate through internet websites a post of your mugshot released by the CCSO. This practice leaves you open to a form of extortion if you ever want to remove it. Why they want to continue this practice makes no sense.

Mine has been posted three and a half years,

damaging my character, employment possibilities,

causing undo pain to my family and it would do the

same to you and yours.

I refuse to pay the exorbitant fees ($2,000)

to remove my picture from the sites and suffer the

consequences of not doing so. You too will face this

form of extortion. www.bailbondsearch.com

RUMMER, JASON, view arrest, jail and bonding information

for this inmate that has been incarcerated at the Collier

County Jail in Naples, FL.

THE MOST IMPORTANT THINGS

TO REMEMBER (IN MY OPINION)

A CCSO Deputy Sherriff has turned their

flashing lights on and you see them in your rear

window or side mirrors.   Please consider the

following when this occurs –

1. USE A TURN SIGNAL AND PULL OFF THE

    ROAD.

2. TURN ON YOUR EMERGENCY FLASHING

    LIGHTS.

3. KEEP YOUR DRIVER'S WINDOW $1/3^{RD}$

    CLOSED.

4. HAVE YOUR DRIVER'S LICENSE, INSURANCE

    AND REGISTRATION READY TO PROVIDE TO

    THE DEPUTY.

5. KEEP YOUR HANDS ON YOUR STEARING WHEEL WHERE THE DEPUTY CAN SEE THEM.

6. WHEN THE DEPUTY ASK'S YOU, "DO YOU KNOW

7. WHY YOU WERE PULLED OVER (STOPPED, ETC.), RESPOND POLITELY THAT YOU DO NOT KNOW WHY, UNLESS IT IS VERY APPARENT WHY YOU WERE (SPEEDING, TRAFFIC SIGNAL VIOLATION, ACCIDENT).

8. DO NOT ADMIT TO HAVING ANYTHING TO DRINK OR SMOKE.

9. DO NOT SUBMIT TO A FIELD SOBRIETY TEST.

10. DO NOT SUBMIT TO A BREATHALYZER TEST

(UNLESS YOU **_REALLY_** ONLY HAD ONE BEER

OR GLASS OF WINE).

11. DON'T BE AFRAID, YOU WILL BE ARRESTED

AND TAKEN TO THE COUNTY JAIL.

YOUR VEHICLE WILL BE TOWED AND YOU WILL BE ABLE TO PICK IT UP THE NEXT DAY. THE COST FOR THE TOW WILL BE $300 OR MORE.

No matter what your impulses of honesty tell you, do not take a field test, a breathalyzer test (do not blow), and stay alert, only answering the questions asked. Doing so, you will lose your Driver's License (DL) for a year (or less) but, can and will (most likely) retain work driving privileges for the entire time.

YOU MUST contact the state approved "Hardship Driver's License" test provider within **10 DAYS FROM ARREST** to gain approval for the Hardship License. The cost at the Florida State Driver's License office will be a minimum of $200.

Your bail will be $1,000 to $5,000. You must pay 10 percent of the bail amount to the bail bonds person or company. The next day you will then be able to defend yourself with a hired private or court provided public attorney or yourself. The state prosecutor will only have a video with audio of your arrest and the Deputy Sherriff's report as evidence to use against you. Since you did not submit to a field sobriety test, breath, or blood alcohol test, this provides a more difficult case to prosecute by the state and may lead to reduced charges such as reckless operation or even no charge.

Watch out for:

1. CCSO motorcycle speed traps on US 41 from Vanderbilt Road south to Pine Ridge Road.

2. Unmarked Ford cars that are the color gray dedicated to a Driving Under the Influence (DUI) "Task Force".

3. Ford and (and Chevy) pickup trucks made out to look like personal vehicles with stickers and such that park at the Vanderbilt Beach Circle.

4. Ford Escapes and Explorer SUVS that search for, "Probable Cause" events in Naples Park, Naples Manor, Golden Gate City and Parkway, Immokalee, Airport Pulling roadway and Everglades City.

5. 101st Street (Naples Park), do not venture on it after 10:00pm as it is a prime CCSO feeding ground and period.

6. Walking home on 101st street in Naples Park late at night.

7. Riding a bicycle late at night.

8. Riding a bicycle that does on have a front or back light.

9. Driving on 8th Avenue in Naples Park late at night.

10. Double pump on your brakes at a stop sign.

11. "Rolling" (not fully stopping) through a stop sign

regulated intersection.

12.   Any (and all) bulbs not functioning on your

vehicles including trailers.

13. Turn signals not being used.

14. License plate lenses (tint darkness).

15. License plates not correctly registered.

16. Too dark of window tint.

CORONA VIRUS Arrest Data

It appears there is a lack of daily arrests during the CORONA VIRUS (CONVID – 19). Comparing the same period from 2019 (both March & April, 30 days) the average arrests (*daily*) for Collier County were eighteen (18) in 2019 and in 2020, were just five (5) on average.

How is this possible? Was, the revenue producing County activity using, "Probable Cause" to create arrests discontinued?

Please keep in mind that 15% of daily arrests in the county are people that live outside the county.

On Tuesday, March 17, 2020, St. Patrick's Day, there were five arrests compared with previous year's average of 17 or 82.4% LESS!

WHAT happened to cause this amazing reduction in arrests? Coronavirus, yes? Less Deputies and Jail LEO's available for work, maybe?

Or was the reduction of arrests, due to direction of the CCSO to not use, "Probable Cause", to create arrests of the Citizens of Collier County or others, and only arrest those how have committed a crime? On the next page are the statistics that the data was arrived from.

CORONAVIRUS (CONVID – 19) ARREST STATISTICS

FROM MARCH 15 THROUGH APRIL 15, 2020

COMPARED TO SAME PERIOD IN 2019.

DAY	MAR & APR YEAR 2019	DAY	COVID-19 3/15 - 4/15/2020	PERCENT % DIFFERENCE YOY
M	19	M	4	-78.9%
TU	20	TU	5	-75.0%
W	18	W	5	-72.2%
TH	22	TH	9	-59.1%
F	16	F	5	-68.8%
SA	16	SA	4	-75.0%
SU	17	SU	4	-76.5%
TOTAL	128	TOTAL	36	-71.9%
AVG. ARRESTS PER DAY	18		5	-72.2%

	Arrest Percent	Population Percent
Caucasian	49.2%	63.6%
African American	24.2%	6.8%
Hispanic/Latino	26.6%	27.2%

The during the period from March 15 through April 15, the Coronavirus, CONVID-19 saw most of the arrests were home burglaries and domestic violence. Over 50 percent. Maybe the Citizens of Collier County are better served using CCSO Deputies to be focused on those issues *instead* of returning to the use of, "Probable Cause Incidents" to create its arrests?

<u>**CCSO MISSION STATEMENT and Final Thoughts**</u>

The duty of the Collier County Sheriff's Office is to preserve and protect the lives, property, and *constitutional guarantees of all persons. The public has the right to efficient, fair, and impartial treatment.* the Professional Responsibility Bureau protects the relationship between the CCSO and the public by investigating all allegations made against CCSO members by the public or any agency member.

Well, there you have it, hopefully a clearer

picture of Collier County Legal from one person's

notes and the representation of many.

Appendix

SAMPLE STATISTICS

DP05: ACS DEMOGRAPHIC AND
2013-2017 American Community Survey

Subject	Collier County, Florida			
	Estimate	Margin of	Percent	Percent
SEX AND AGE				
Total population	356,774	*****	356,774	(X)
Male	175,608	+/-102	49.2%	+/-0.1
Female	181,166	+/-102	50.8%	+/-0.1
Total population	356,774	*****	356,774	(X)
Hispanic or Latino (of any race)	**96,948**	*****	**27.2%**	*****
White alone	**227,002**	**+/-270**	**63.6%**	+/-0.1
Black or African American alone	**24,395**	**+/-424**	**6.8%**	+/-0.1
Total housing units	207,403	+/-284	(X)	(X)

ZIP CODE TARGETING					
	Jul-17	**Arrest**		**Aug-17**	**Arrest**
34142	Immokalee	61	34142	Immokalee	57
34141	Everglades	1	34141	Everglades	1
34138	Chokoloskee	2	34138	Chokoloskee	3
34139	Everglades City	2	34139	Everglades City	2
34137	Copeland	5	34137	Copeland	1
34120	Fairgrounds	26	34120	Fairgrounds	35
34117	Estates	15	34117	Estates	26
34114	East Naples	13	34114	East Naples	15
34140	Goodland	1	34140	Goodland	1
34145	Marco Island	5	34145	Marco Island	14
34113	South Naples	40	34113	South Naples	25
34112	Airport Pulling	68	34112	Airport Pulling	53
34102	Naples	9	34102	Naples	9
34104	Goodlette Frank	24	34104	Goodlette	27
34116	Golden Gate	60	34116	Golden Gate	63
34119	Livingston	12	34119	Livingston	9
34105	Pine Ridge	11	34105	Pine Ridge	14
34103	Seagate	9	34103	Seagate	12
34109	Pelican Marsh	10	34109	Pelican Marsh	13
34108	Naples Park	26	34108	Naples Park	20
34119	Immokalee Rd	2	34119	Immokalee Rd	5
34110	North Naples	16	34110	North Naples	10
		418			**415**

DATE	W	B	H	ZIP
12/20/19	9	3	7	(2) 113, (2) 115, 103, 105, 137, (3) 142, 120
12/21/19	9	3	7	102, 104, (3) 142, 109, (5) 116, 119, (2) 103, 108, 113
12/22/19	3	0	2	142, 116, 113
12/23/19	6	7	7	(3) 142, 112, 105, 102, 139, 114, (2) 116
12/24/19	8	2	6	(2) 114, 108, 112, (6) 142, 145, 104
12/25/19	5	4	6	(5) 112, (3) 116, (3) 142, 119, 114, 117
12/26/19	9	1	4	(3) 116, (2) 112, 102, 113, (2) 120, 117, (2) 142, 110
12/27/19	9	5	7	110, (4) 113, (2) 112, (2) 116, 120, 142, (2) 120
12/28/19	4	0	7	(2) 112, (2) 116, (2) 142, 114
12/29/19	4	4	4	116, (2) 120, 110, (2) 112, 104, 108, 142, 119
12/30/19	7	0	1	108, 116, 112, (2) 104, (2) 113,
12/31/19	13	6	4	(3) 113, (4)114, 103, 112, (2) 116, (4) 142, 120
1/1/20	9	3	8	(2) 120, (3) 142, 104, (3) 116, 109, (2) 102, 114, 113
1/2/20	9	2	2	113, (2) 116, 119, (3) 112,
1/3/20	14	4	6	104, (3) 119, 103, (2) 142, (2) 112, (2) 120, (2) 113, 108, 102, 116
1/4/20	10	3	2	(3) 112, 142, 145, 113, 114, 109, 119, 108, 106
1/5/20	5	2	6	112, (2) 113, (2) 142, (2) (2) 120, (2) 116,
1/6/20	9	1	3	N/A
1/7/20	13	4	7	108, 102, (2) 142, (2) 103, (3) 113, 104, (3) 112, (3) 114, 117, 116, 109, 120
1/8/20	9	3	6	110, (4) 112, 142, 119, (2) 108, 113, 114, 116, 103, 102, 120
1/9/20	10	3	2	139, (2) 116, (2) 119, 114, (2) 112, (2) 104, 113,
1/10/20	7	3	8	(2) 109, 116, 110, (3) 113, (3) 142, 139, 104, 120,
1/11/20	11	1	4	(2) 116, (3) 142, (4) 104, (2) 112, 114, 108, 119
1/12/20	10	4	3	(2) 120, 112, (2) 116, 102, (2) 142, 103, 117, 108,
1/13/20	16	4	6	(2) 114, 104, (2) 113, (4) 112, 145, (4) 120, 105, 142, (2) 117
1/14/20	11	4	9	145, (2) 113, (2) 112, (2) 116, (2) 142, 117, 104, 139, 104
1/15/20	13	4	4	109, (5) 142, 135, 105, 119, 104, 114, (2) 112, (2) 109, 145, 113
1/16/20	11	2	7	(3) 120,104,108, 142, (2) 112, (2) 113, (2) 116, (3) 114, 119
1/17/20	14	3	2	104, 113, (2) 110, (3) 109, 112, 120, 117, (2) 142
1/18/20	2	2	5	(3) 142, 114, 104, 108,
1/19/20	7	1	7	(2) 112, 120, (2) 104, 119, 142, 117, 114,
	276	**88**	**159**	
TOTAL	**523**			
ARREST %	52.8%	16.8%	30.4%	

218

RULE 3.220. DISCOVERY

(a) Notice of Discovery.

After the filing of the charging document, a defendant may elect to participate in the discovery process provided by these rules, including the taking of discovery depositions, by filing with the court and serving on the prosecuting attorney a "Notice of Discovery" which shall bind both the prosecution and defendant to all discovery procedures contained in these rules.

(b) Prosecutor's Discovery Obligation.

(1) Within 15 days after service of the Notice of Discovery, the prosecutor shall serve a written

Discovery Exhibit which shall disclose to the defendant and permit the defendant to inspect, copy, test, and photograph the following information and material within the state's possession or control, or otherwise reproduced so long as the state attorney makes the property or material reasonably available to the defendant or the defendant's attorney:

(c) Disclosure to Prosecution.

(1) After the filing of the charging document and subject to constitutional limitations, the court may require a defendant to:

(d) Defendant's Obligation.

(1) If a defendant elects to participate in discovery, either through filing the appropriate notice or by participating in any discovery process, including the taking of a discovery deposition, the following disclosures shall be made:

(A) Within 15 days after receipt by the defendant of the Discovery Exhibit furnished by the prosecutor pursuant to subdivision (b)(1)(A) of this rule, the defendant shall furnish to the prosecutor a written list of the names and addresses of all witnesses whom the defendant expects to call as witnesses at the trial or hearing. When the prosecutor subpoenas a witness, whose name has been furnished by the defendant, except for trial subpoenas, the rules applicable to the taking of depositions shall apply.

Self-Incrimination

The Fifth Amendment protects criminal defendants from having to testify if they may incriminate themselves through the testimony. A witness may "plead the Fifth" and not answer if the witness believes answering the question may be self-incriminatory.

- In the landmark *Miranda v. Arizona* ruling, the United States Supreme Court extended the Fifth Amendment protections to encompass any situation outside of the courtroom that involves the curtailment of personal freedom. 384 U.S. 436 (1966).

Therefore, any time that law enforcement takes a suspect into custody, law enforcement must make the suspect aware of all rights. Known as *Miranda* rights, these rights include the right to remain silent, the right to have an attorney present during questioning, and the right to have a government-appointed attorney if the suspect cannot afford one.

Probable cause

In Florida, there are several statutes related to the application of probable cause. **Generally, a law enforcement officer must observe events that lead him or her to determine that probable cause**

exists. Otherwise, a law enforcement officer generally needs to convince a judge to issue an arrest warrant. However, a law enforcement officer can arrest someone without having observed any events and without an arrest warrant if that officer determines that the person has committed a criminal act under one of the following statutes:

- <u>Florida Statute 790.233</u>: related to possession of ammunition, firearms, or when a person is subject to injunctions against committing acts of stalking, domestic violence, or cyberstalking

- <u>Florida Statute 741.31</u>: related to violation of an injunction for a domestic violence protection order

- <u>Florida Statute 784.07</u>: related to violating a protective order for sexual violence, repeat violence, or sexual violence.

Definitions –

- **Absentia**

  Absent; proceeding without defendant being present.

- **Acquittal**

  A finding of not guilty by judge or jury.

- **Adjudication**

  A judgment rendered by the court after a finding of guilt.

- **Affidavit of Insolvency**

  A form signed by the defendant under oath attesting to inability to pay.

- **Answer to Demand**

  A document filed by the State Attorney\'s Office responding to a demand for discovery by a defense attorney, setting forth witnesses in the case, information about the case, and allowing duplication of case information/reports.

- **Appeal**

  An application, lodged by the defendant or the State Attorney\'s Office, requesting a review of the case by the court of appeal.

- **Arraignment**

  Appearance of the defendant in court to enter his/her plea to charges.

- **Assistant State Attorney**

  State employee designated by the State Attorney to prosecute defendants.

- **Attorney of Record**

  The attorney retained/assigned to represent a client.

- **Bail**

  Cash or surety posted to procure the release of a defendant and to ensure his or her future appearance in court, compelling him/her to remain in the jurisdiction of the court.

- **Bench Warrant**

  Issued by the judge when a defendant fails to appear for a scheduled court appearance.

- **Bond – Surety**

  A certificate posted by a bonding company to the sheriff releasing defendant.

- **Capias**

  A writ to the Sheriff to arrest an accused person.

- **Capias – Instanter**

  Issuance of the arrest order with court direction to bring the accused before court immediately with no bond.

- **Certified Copy**

  A document that is authenticated, signed, and sealed by the Clerk of Court.

- **Challenge**

  Term used in a jury trial when attempting to excuse a juror.

- **Charging Document**

  A Citation, Information, Indictment, Petition, or Notice to Appear indicating that the named person is accused of committing a specific criminal offense or civil infraction.

- **Citation**

  The summons handed to defendant indicating the offense committed.

- **Clerk of Court**

  County office that receives all original paperwork on each criminal case.

- **Community Control**

  Form of probation restricting defendant\'s movements.

- **Contempt of Court**

  Act of disrespect to the court; willful disregard of court\'s authority.

- **Continuance**

  Postponing a trial or hearing to a later date.

- **Court Date Notice**

  A written form used to bring the accused to court.

- **County Court**

  The court that hears misdemeanor, traffic cases, municipal ordinance violations, etc.

- **Court Reporter**

  Maintains a verbatim record of court events.

- **Defendant**

  Person accused of a crime.

- **Deferred Payment**

  Court grants additional time to pay a fine.

- **Demand for Discovery**

  Demand by the defense attorney to the State Attorney to furnish material information on a case.

- **Deposition**

  Questioning of a witness before a court reporter by an opposing counsel as part of pretrial discovery process.

- **Directed Verdict**

  Dismissed by a judge.

- **Dismissed**

  Dismissed by a judge.

  Dispositions

  The final action of a case.

- **Discharge of Bond**

  A court order to release bond, usually once the case is disposed.

- **Docket**

  A list of cases pending before the court.

- **Evidence Log**

  A list of all items entered as evidence in trial (exhibits).

- **Exhibits**

  Any paper or object offered in court that is marked for identification or evidence.

- **Expungement**

  Destroy, obliterate, and wholly strike out the criminal history record of a person's case.

- **Felony**

  Crime carrying a penalty of possible incarceration in state prison. (one year +)

- **File/Record**

  The Clerk\'s office\'s official recording of minutes and all documents signed by the judge.

- **First Appearance**

  Accused's right to see a judge within 24 hours of arrest.

- **Florida Statutes**

  A listing or book of the laws of the state of Florida.

- **Fugitive**

  A person who flees from one state to another to avoid prosecution.

- **Habeas Corpus**

  A means to bring the defendant before the court to determine whether he/she is being detained unlawfully.

- **Hearing Proceedings**

  Record of testimony/evidence entered.

- **Incarceration**

  Confinement in prison/jail.

- **Indictment**

  A formal charging document issued by a Grand Jury to the Court wherein the named person(s) is accused of committing a specific crime.

- **Indigent**

  A defendant unable to afford a private defense attorney. These clients are represented by the public defender or a conflict attorney.

- **Information**

  A formal charging document issued by the State Attorney wherein the named person is accused of committing a specific offense.

- **Initial Proceedings**

  The first court appearance of a defendant on a charge.

- **Intake**

  Process by which the State Attorney makes up a criminal file, files upon the case, etc.

- **Judgment/Sentence**

  The official document of a judge\'s disposition (decision) of a case and sentence of a defendant.

- **Jurisdiction**

  The authority/power to hear a case.

- **Jury Trial**

  A trial in which a jury decides the facts at issue.

- **Misdemeanor**

  An offense punishable by not more than one year in jail and a $1,000 fine.

- **Motion**

  A document filed with the court requesting an order or ruling in favor of the applicant.

- **Motion to Seal**

  A motion to close a record to public inspection.

- **Motion to Suppress**

  A motion to prevent admission of evidence

  in a case.

- **No Contest/Nolo Contendere**

  A defendant neither admits nor denies the

  charges, letting them stand as is.

- **No Probable Cause**

  Insufficient grounds to hold the person who

  was arrested.

- **Non-Jury Trial**

  A case tried by a judge.

- **Oaths**

  Sworn attestations required in court.

- **Oath of Indigency and Order Appointing
  Counsel**

  A document signed by the defendant under

oath before the judge stating he/she is without funds to retain an attorney. The judge may then declare the defendant indigent and sign an order appointing counsel.

- **Order**

  A document signed by the judge making an award or ruling.

- **Petition**

  A formal charging document issued by the State Attorney wherein the named juvenile is accused of committing a specific offense.

Plaintiff

The one bringing the charges against the accused, generally in a civil case.

- **Plea**

  Defendant\'s answer to the charge.

- **Plea Negotiations**

  Negotiations between the State and the

  defense for a fair disposition of the case

  and requiring approval of the court.

- **Pre-Trial Intervention**

  A county program to aid certain qualified

  defendants by diverting them from court

  proceedings upon successful completion of

  the program.

- **Probable Cause**

  Reasonable belief that a crime was

  committed and that the named person

  committed the crime.

- **Pre-Trial Release**

  Release of a defendant after arrest and before any court appearance date.

- **Probation**

  Suspension of a sentence, with or without adjudication of guilt, and placing the defendant under supervision of the Department of Corrections Probation and Parole Services for a specified period, and with conditions of behavior.

- **Public Defender**

  A court appointed attorney for those defendants who are declared indigent.

- **Recusal**

  A judge excuses himself from

hearing/considering a case due to some conflict.

- **Record/File**

The Clerk\'s office\'s official recording of minutes and all documents signed by the judge.

- **Sealing a criminal record**

To close a criminal record, make unavailable, confidential, or exempt from public record.

- **Sentence/Judgment**

The official document of a judge\'s disposition (decision) of a case and sentence of a defendant.

- **Show Cause Order**

An order issued by the court requiring a

person to appear and show why some action should not be taken.

- **Speedy Trial**

  A rule of law wherein the defendant must be brought to trial within 90 days for misdemeanor and 175 days for felony charge(s).

- **Statement of Particulars**

  A detailed statement of the offense charged, enough to enable the defendant to properly prepare his/her defense.

- **Subpoena Duces Tecum**

  Court process requiring a witness to produce requested documents or other materials, at a specific time/date.

- **Summons**

  A document signed by a deputy clerk
  ordering a person to appear before the
  court.

- **Sworn Complaint Affidavit**

  A sworn, witnessed complaint filed with the
  Clerk of Court initiating a criminal case.

- **Time Served**

  Actual number of days served in jail.

- **Verdict**

  The findings of a judge or jury at the end of
  a trial.

- **Voir Dire**

  Examination of a jury panel by the judge,
  defense counsel, and the State Attorney for
  selection to serve on a case.

- **Warrant**

  A writ issued by a judge authorizing an
  officer to make an arrest, a seizure, or a
  search, or to do other acts incident to the
  administration of justice.

- **Withhold of Adjudication**

  The judge withholds the judgment of
  guilt/conviction on an offense.

- **Writ**

  A written document/order requiring the
  performance of a specified act or giving
  authority and commission to have it done.

- **Written Plea of Not Guilty**

  A defendant\'s plea in writing to the court.
  In the felony court, this plea may only be
  filed by counsel.

Writer and Researcher – Jason Rummer

59, born in 1960, moved thirty-three times (NYC, Seattle, Dallas, Nashville, and the Midwest) due to his family and work commitments. He a father of three daughters, two married college graduates (one a cancer survivor) living in Louisiana. The youngest is with him in Naples, Florida. Five fiancés, three marriages, and a widower. He has survived over ninety-nine, "life" time events and this is his third published work.

www.ingramcontent.com/pod-product-compliance
Lightning Source LLC
Chambersburg PA
CBHW051438250726
48655CB00001B/117